Make Your Own

SUPER SQUISHIES SLIME AND PUTTY

First edition for the United States and Canada published in 2018 by
Barron's Educational Series, Inc.

All inquiries should be addressed to:
Barron's Educational Series, Inc.
250 Wireless Boulevard
Hauppauge, NY 11788
www.barronseduc.com

Publisher: Mark Searle
Associate Publisher: Emma Bastow
Commissioning Editor: Sorrel Wood
Managing Editor: Isheeta Mustafi
Editors: Jane Roe and Abbie Sharman
Art Director: Katherine Radcliffe
Design: Lynsey Gray
Photography: Simon Pask

ISBN: 978-1-4380-1253-7
Library of Congress Control Number: 2018938681

Date of Manufacture: April 2018

Manufactured by: 1010 Printing International Limited, North Point, Hong Kong

Printed in China

9 8 7 6 5 4 3 2 1

FSC
www.fsc.org

MIX
Paper from
responsible sources
FSC® C016973

Disclaimer: The projects in this book are not edible. Always follow manufacturer's
instructions for safe use and disposal of materials and ingredients. The publisher
does not accept responsibility for any injuries or accidents.

Make Your Own

SUPER SQUISHIES

SLIME AND PUTTY

36 Easy Projects to Make!

Tessa Sillars-Powell

BARRON'S

Contents

How to Make Squishies

How to Make Slime

How to Make Putty

Introduction

Welcome to the world of **SQUISHIES, SLIME, AND PUTTY,** a place to de-stress, find inner satisfaction, and ultimately be surrounded by cute and squishy things. Where did our obsession come from? What is it that is so mesmerizing about squishies? And what do they all have in common?!

For the uninitiated, **SQUISHIES** are soft, squeezable toys, similar to stress balls, only much cuter. It's their super squishy nature that gives them their name. The magic is in the squishy's slow rise back into its formed shape, however squished it gets—the slower the rise back, the more pleasing it is.

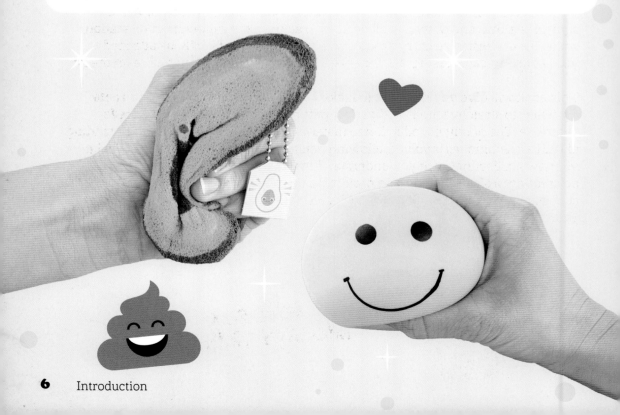

SLIME! A fascinating concoction of ingredients that, when mixed, create a satisfying, oozing glob of slime, which stretches, snaps, melts, and molds. It has to be seen to be believed.

PUTTY is squidgy like slime, but unlike slime it is easier to mold and keeps its shape. Like a soft playdough, it can be calming to squeeze, squelch, and shape.

So why?! When playing with squishies, slime, and putty, the repetitive action relieves excess energy, distracting your brain from stress in a similar way to meditation. The rest of your attention can then be used elsewhere, allowing you to focus better, think more clearly, retain information, and calm down. While squishies, slime, and putty can all be used to achieve the same sort of relaxation, squishies are easiest to carry around with you as they can easily be attached to your phone or bag, making them the perfect comfort object when you're on the go.

This book will give you the skills to make your very own creations—from cute squishies to stretchy slimes and perfect putties, there is something in here for everyone. The handy introduction to materials will give you a solid understanding of the key techniques involved, allowing you to think outside the box and design your own collection; once you understand that the possibilities are endless you'll be creating professional-looking projects in no time. Be sure to check out the cool labels on pages 108–109, too, which can be used to give your end pieces that showstopping "off the shelf" finish.

**HAVE FUN
AND STAY SQUISHY!**

The Basics

Squishies

Store-bought squishies are made from a special type of heat-molded foam; however, when you're making them at home, there are a few different methods and materials you can use, all with their own advantages. Some of these are everyday materials that you probably already have at home. For other materials, you may need to visit your local craft store or buy them online. Most importantly though, any of the designs in this book can be adjusted to suit your preferences and your available materials, so while I've provided step-by-step instructions to start you off, don't think that there are any boundaries. Once you understand the key techniques and materials detailed below, there'll be no end to your squishy fun!

There are three main methods when creating DIY squishies—carving foam or sponge, filling balloons, or making paper squishies—and through trying them all you'll find your favorite technique. Sometimes you've just got to go with the materials you already have when you just NEED to make a squishy in a rush, so always try and be inventive and think outside the box.

SPONGE/FOAM SQUISHIES

Sponges

From car-washing and dish-washing sponges to bath sponges, anything spongy is good for making squishies. They are readily available from supermarkets and come in a variety of sizes; you can also find them in different colors, which can make a good base for your design.

Warning: Scissors are used in a number of projects—adult supervision is recommended.

Makeup sponges

For smaller squishies, makeup sponges can provide a good base as they come in a variety of preformed shapes and styles. They are slow rising, and have very smooth surfaces that hold paint well. They can be found in most cosmetic stores and online.

Memory foam

This is really squishy and great for making slow-rise squishies. It can be easily cut and shaped, and its density means it holds paint well, too. You can easily pick up offcuts as you don't need much for standard-size squishies, and it can also be found in memory foam pillows.

Puffy paint

This special 3-D puffy paint coats sponges and foam. It gives them good coverage while retaining their flexibility. Since it is thick it covers up any holes and smooths any mistakes made when carving. It is available in most craft stores and online.

DIY puffy paint

You can make your own puffy paint by mixing two parts paint to one part glue. Stir well and apply as normal.

Fabric paint

This can be a good substitute for puffy paint. It gives good coverage and dries flexible, but it's not as thick as puffy paint so you have to be happy with the surface before you paint it—fabric paint won't hide any imperfections! It is available in most craft stores and online.

Paint mixing

By mixing your paints you'll be able to create a wide range of colors for your projects. This is really useful as it means you don't need to buy every color. Use this color wheel to help you mix up a rainbow!

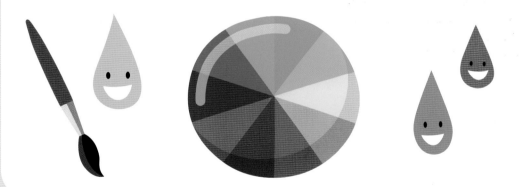

Gloves

Latex gloves keep your hands clean and allow you to use your hands to easily spread the paint on the foam.

Markers

Use permanent markers, ballpoint pens, or chalk markers to add details.

BALLOON SQUISHIES

Balloons

The balloon method creates smooth results and is quick to do. Balloon squishies are particularly satisfying to squish because of their cornstarch filling. Balloons are easy to come by and are available in a range of colors, meaning you have free rein to create many different looking squishies. You may even be able to find shaped balloons, which will take your projects to the next level!

Cornstarch

The key filling to a balloon squishy is cornstarch. Because it is finer than regular flour, it has a smoother texture and therefore squishes better.

Markers

Make sure you use permanent markers so your designs don't smudge.

Warning: Scissors are used in a number of projects—adult supervision is recommended.

PAPER SQUISHIES

Paper

The great thing about paper squishies is that you probably have the materials right under your nose. As the main material is paper, you can easily decorate it with any design using just markers and colored pencils, meaning there is no waiting for it to dry and you can quickly get squishing. Regular white paper works well for these.

Stuffing

All paper squishies need stuffing. You can experiment with what gives you the best rise back. Basically anything that's squishy will work! Cotton wool, toy stuffing, cut-up grocery bags, and shredded tissues are just some of the things you can use. They are all easy to come by, and give a smooth filling and a satisfying squish.

How to package your squishies

One of the key things in creating your own squishies is packaging them to look professionally made. This makes them all the more impressive when showing them to your friends or gifting them, and it can be done simply yet effectively.

Labels

Nothing finishes off a project better than a well-designed label. On page 108 you'll find some to either photocopy or trace, but you can design your own, too. Use thin card paper and either colored pencils or markers to make them. Cut the label out and fold it in half, slide a ball chain into the label, and tape the label ends together.

Ball chains

These little clip-together chains come in a variety of lengths and can be used to attach your squishies to anything from a backpack to a spiral notebook. There is a good chance you might already have one on a toy or accessory, or they can be easily bought online.

Rubber bands

If you don't have access to a ball chain these can be an easy substitute, plus they're stretchy, which makes squishing on the go even easier!

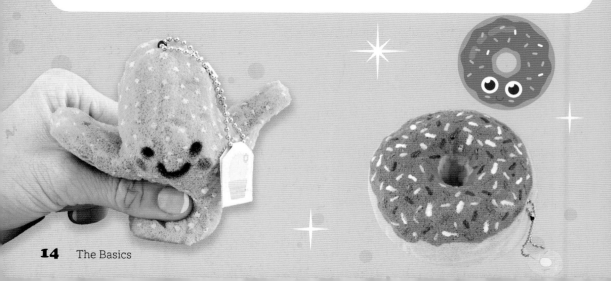

Bobby pins

The great thing about sliding your rubber band or ball chain into a bobby pin is that you can then easily poke it into your squishy and remove it, too. If you want it to be permanently secured, use a small amount of glue on its tip to hold it in place. You can also use a wooden skewer to create a small hole for the bobby pin.

Clear ziplock bags

When gifting your squishies, give them that extra store-bought quality by labeling and then sealing them inside a clear ziplock bag. This will also keep them looking new and fresh.

Boxes

Certain projects look great in boxes. You can either find an existing box and decorate it, or make your own. To make your own box, cut a square from a piece of thin card paper, and decorate it. Then, use the template on page 110 to assemble the box.

Slime

Slime can be made in many ways—try a few different techniques to find your favorite. These recipes aim to be low mess, and also mainly use things you may already have around the house. The slimes fall into three categories, standard slime, fluffy slime, and clear slime, but they all share some common ingredients.

White glue
Also known as school glue, PVA glue, or just glue, for the purpose of this it's all the same! Different slimers have preferences for different brands, it is all about finding one that works for you.

Clear glue
This can be used to make clear slimes, jelly slimes, and liquid glass slimes. Any slime made with clear glue will be extra shiny. Be sure to use a nontoxic variety.

Baking soda
Also known as bicarbonate of soda, this works as a reactor to make your slime slime!

Contact lens solution
This should contain boric acid for your slime to form. Because it is designed to come into contact with skin, boric acid is perfectly safe to be added to the mixture in this diluted form.

Storage
Store your slime in an airtight container or ziplock bag. Keeping it in the refrigerator can also help it stay fresh.

Gloves
Latex gloves can be useful for keeping your hands clean, especially if you have sensitive skin.

Shaving cream
This makes your slime super light and fluffy. A little goes a long way.

Food coloring
You can either use gel or liquid coloring to make your projects a lot more exciting.

Putty

Putty, being more moldable than slime, is generally thicker and drier to mix. This means it should be cleaner to make and is just as satisfying! There isn't as much variation in the methods of creating putty but that's not to say you can't experiment! One of the key ways to do this is by adding fragrances or essential oils, which can make putties particularly relaxing to play with.

Flour

This thickens your putty. When cornstarch is mixed with water it forms a special type of fluid that responds to being stirred and squeezed differently depending on how quickly the force is applied. Both cornstarch and regular flour will work, though each will have a slightly different texture.

Salt

This gives body to your putty and keeps it fresher longer.

Oil

This gives your putty a really nice soft, smooth feel when you play with it and generally holds it together better without cracking.

Storage

Store your putty in an airtight container or ziplock bag. Keeping it in the refrigerator can also help it stay fresh.

Now that you understand the principles of squishies, slime, and putty, it's time to get creative. There's a selection of projects over the next 100 pages to get you started. Remember to keep your work area clean, your mind squishy, and most of all, have fun!

How to Make Squishies

Get squishing!

BURGER

BURGER TIME!

This squishy has a fun texture as it's covered in a surprising material—pantyhose! This means the sponge stays extra squishy and it has a smoother finish that looks extra professional. You can add any craft foam toppings you like to take it to the next level. The box works really well as a finishing touch, making it the perfect gift.

Materials:

Black marker
Sponge
Craft foam in yellow, red, and green
Pantyhose
Puffy paints in white, yellow, green, and red
Box (instructions on page 110)
Double-sided tape

Tools:

Scissors
Paintbrush

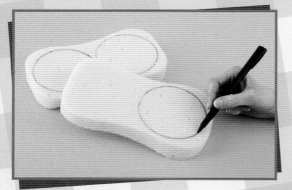

1 Cut your sponge in half height-wise. Use a marker to draw three circles onto the pieces.

Trace around something circular to get a good shape for your burger!

2 Cut the circles out and carefully trim two of them into bun shapes and one into a burger shape. Remember, the top bun is curved, the bottom bun is flat!

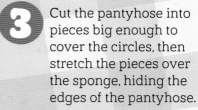

3 Cut the pantyhose into pieces big enough to cover the circles, then stretch the pieces over the sponge, hiding the edges of the pantyhose.

4 Mix red, yellow, green, and white puffy paint to create a bread color and paint over the bun pieces. Once the paint is dry, add sesame seed details with white puffy paint on the top bun. Mix green and red puffy paint to make brown, and paint the burger.

Turn the page!

Burger   **23**

5

Cut a yellow piece of craft foam for the cheese, a red piece for the tomatoes, and a green piece for the lettuce.

6

Stick all of the layers together using double-sided tape. For a finishing touch, draw a face and sesame seeds on the top bun, then put the burger in the box.

PSST! You can make me, too, on the next page!

HE'S SO CUTE!

NOW SQUISH IT!

Make the box following the template on page 110.

FRIES

An iconic classic, this great-looking project can be made in a few easy steps. Using the natural color of the sponge for the fries means that you don't have any tricky painting to do, and the texture looks nice and crispy. When you squeeze the packet, the fries pop out for an extra satisfying twist!

Materials:

Black marker
Sponge
Puffy paints in red and yellow
Bobby pin
Ball chain (optional)
Label (from page 109)
Tape

Tools:

Scissors
Paintbrush

1 Draw a slightly angled rectangle onto your sponge and cut it out.

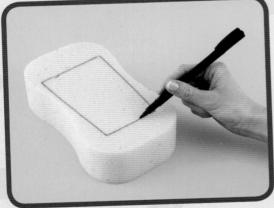

2 Cut one-third of the way down from the wider top part of the sponge to create rectangular shapes. Trim some of your "fries" to different lengths to make them look more realistic.

3 Use red puffy paint to paint the uncut sides to look like the fries box.

4 Once dry, use yellow puffy paint to add details to the box.

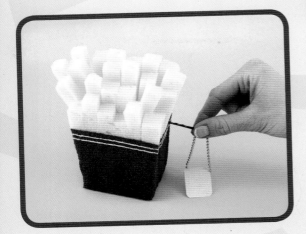

5 Use tape to attach your label to the ball chain, and then slide the chain into the bobby pin. Push the bobby pin into the sponge to finish.

Panda

Simple to create, this super-smooth panda is satisfying to squish and pleasing to poke. You can decorate it with any expression you desire, giving you the opportunity to really get creative. Why not make a panda family in different sizes?

Squish it!

Materials:
White balloon
1 cup cornstarch
Black and pink markers
Ball chain (optional)
Label (from page 109)
Tape

Tools:
Funnel
Plastic bottle (empty, clean, and dry)
Scissors

1 Using the funnel, pour the cornstarch into the bottle.

2 Inflate the balloon slightly and stretch it over the neck of the bottle.

3 Tip the bottle upside down to pour all the cornstarch into the balloon. Remove it from the bottle, release the excess air, and tie a knot at the opening.

4 Use the black marker to draw eyes, a nose, and a mouth, and add a tongue with the pink marker.

5 Finally, use tape to attach your label to the ball chain. Make a tiny snip in the neck of the balloon, and poke the chain through, clipping to secure.

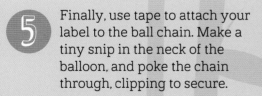

Tip!

For additional security, squeeze the finished ball into a second balloon after step 3. See page 73 for instructions.

Doughnut

This super cute doughnut squishy looks realistic and is really easy to make. The memory foam makes it slow release, giving you that satisfying rise back once squished. You can get really creative with the "frosting" to make your favorite flavor, or make a whole collection to fill a doughnut box. This one is a strawberry rainbow sprinkles design, but there is literally no limit to how you could decorate yours!

Materials:

Black marker
Memory foam
Puffy paints in yellow, white, red, pink, purple, and turquoise
Bobby pin
Ball chain (optional)
Label (from page 109)
Tape

Tools:

Scissors
Paintbrushes

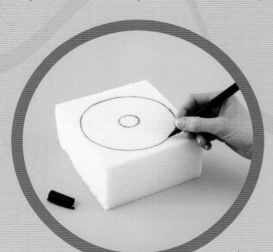

1 Draw a circle on your memory foam with a smaller circle inside it.

To make the doughnut hole, push your scissors through the smaller circle. Then, pick out pieces of foam with your fingers.

2 Cut out the larger circle, rounding off the edges. Next, use your scissors to smooth out the doughnut hole.

3 Mix yellow, white, and a touch of red puffy paint into a dough color and cover the foam with it, then leave to dry.

4 Add pink puffy paint to the top of the doughnut to look like frosting, then add dashes of other colors on top for sprinkles.

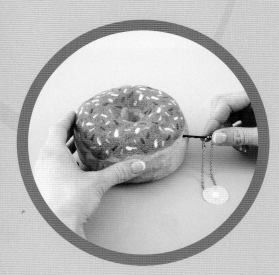

5 When the paint is fully dry, use tape to attach your label to the ball chain, and then slide the chain into the bobby pin. Push the bobby pin into the foam to finish.

PIECE OF CAKE

A piece of cake by name and nature! This project uses makeup sponges as its base, but if you can't get these then sponge or foam will work just as well. The great thing about the makeup sponges is that they have a preformed shape, meaning they have smooth sides and are ready to decorate, saving lots of time. You can try making any variety of cake—this one is a layer cake!

Materials:
2 makeup sponge wedges
Puffy paints in brown, white, pink, and turquoise
Bobby pin
Ball chain (optional)
Label (from page 109)
Tape

Tools:
Scissors
Paintbrushes

1 Stick the two makeup sponges together using white puffy paint and leave to dry.

2 Mix brown and white puffy paint into a cake color and cover the sides and the bottom of the sponge with it, and then leave to dry.

3 Use white puffy paint to look like frosting on the top and back of the wedge. Paint a line halfway up along both sides to look like cream filling, then leave to dry.

4 Add different puffy paint colors on the top and the back to look like sprinkles.

5 When the paint is fully dry, use tape to attach your label to the ball chain, and then slide the chain into the bobby pin. Push the bobby pin into the sponge to finish.

AVOCADO

Who doesn't love an avocado?! This adorable squishy version is just as satisfying to smush as the real thing, and it is just as irresistible with its cute smiley face. Why not try making the other half for your best friend, so you have something to squish even when you are apart!

Materials:

Black marker
Memory foam
Puffy paints in white, yellow, green, brown, and pink
Bobby pin
Ball chain (optional)
Label (from page 108)
Tape

Tools:

Scissors
Paintbrushes

 1 Draw an avocado shape onto your memory foam.

TIP

Alternatively, use an egg-shaped makeup sponge and carefully cut it in half—this will give your project a perfectly smooth finish.

2

Use the scissors to cut out the shape. Curve the back of the avocado, making sure it is smooth.

3

Mix white, yellow, and green puffy paint, then use it to paint the flat side of the foam. Mix a slightly darker shade of green to paint around the edges. Paint the curved side with darker green puffy paint, too.

TURN THE PAGE

4

Use brown puffy paint to make a circle on the flat side for the avocado pit.

5

Once fully dry, use a black marker to add a smiley face, and pink puffy paint to create rosy cheeks on the flat side.

6

Use tape to attach your label to the ball chain, and then slide the chain into the bobby pin. Push the bobby pin into the sponge to finish.

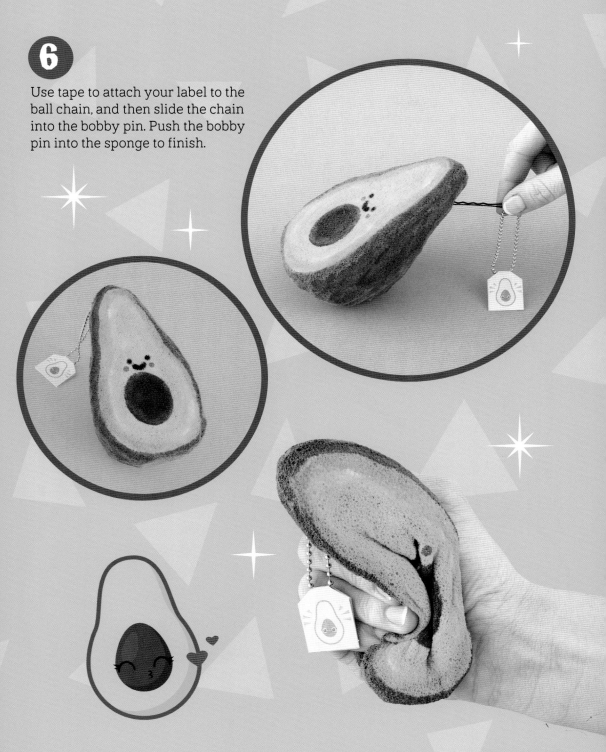

SUSHI

These are really quick to make; once the base is made they can be decorated with any type of filling. They can then be displayed as a collection in a homemade sushi box, and you can squish them with chopsticks if you're feeling adventurous and fancy!

Materials:

Black marker
Memory foam
Puffy paints in dark green and white, plus additional colors for the sushi fillings
Box (instructions on page 110)
Chopsticks

Tools:

Scissors
Paintbrushes

1

Draw a circle on your memory foam and use the scissors to cut it out.

Trace around something circular to get a good shape for your sushi rolls!

2

Paint the edges with dark green puffy paint to look like seaweed, and leave to dry.

3 Paint the top and the bottom with white puffy paint to look like rice.

4 Next, use different colors to paint fillings in your sushi rolls.

5 Repeat the process, getting experimental with the fillings, to create enough sushi to fill your box.

Banana

This silly banana has an incredible texture and is fun to squeeze into different shapes. It's really simple to make, and the craft foam peel really completes the look. You can make the banana any size you want with different balloons—you'd be bananas not to give it a try!

Materials:

Long balloon
1 cup cornstarch
Yellow craft foam
Black masking tape
Black and pink markers

Tools:

Plastic bottle (empty, clean, and dry)
Funnel
Scissors

1 Use the funnel to pour the cornstarch into the plastic bottle. Inflate your balloon slightly, and stretch the neck of the balloon over the neck of the bottle.

2 Turn the bottle upside down and let all of the cornstarch pour into the balloon. Remove it from the bottle, let excess air out, and tie a knot at the opening.

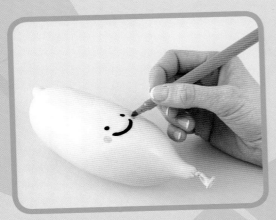

3 Use the markers to decorate it with a face and rosy cheeks.

4 Cut four long leaf shapes out of the yellow craft foam, making sure the combined width of them fits around the balloon. This is the banana peel!

5 Use black masking tape to attach the banana peel around one end of the balloon.

I find you a-peeling!

WATERMELON

This refreshing squishy brings a slice of summer to your day. It's simple to make and easy to change the size of your slice to your taste. The slow-rise memory foam makes it super satisfying to squeeze, especially because it looks so juicy!

Materials:

Black marker
Memory foam
Puffy paints in green, white, red, and black
Bobby pin
Ball chain (optional)
Label (from page 108)
Tape

Tools:

Scissors
Paintbrush

1 Draw one-quarter of a circle shape onto your memory foam.

Trace around something circular to get a good curve for your watermelon!

2 Cut out the shape, and curve off the edges slightly to smooth it out.

3 Use green puffy paint to paint the curved edge, and slightly overlap the sides to suggest a thick watermelon skin. Add a white line beneath the skin to look like the start of the flesh.

4 Paint the rest of the shape with red puffy paint and leave the whole thing to dry.

5 Next, use black paint to add a smiley face and seeds on the flat side. Mix red and white paint to create pink, and give your creation rosy cheeks.

6 Use tape to attach your label to the ball chain, and then slide the chain into the bobby pin. Push the bobby pin into the memory foam to finish.

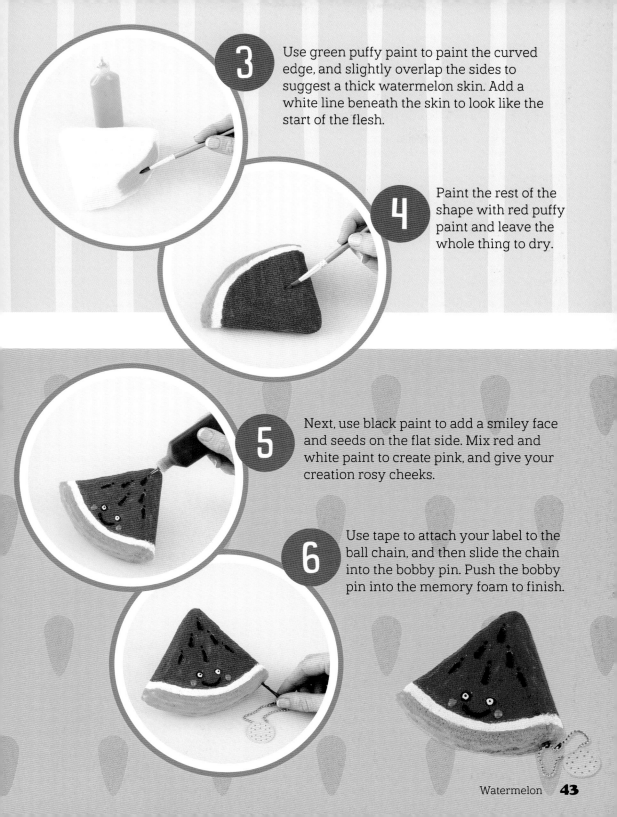

Watermelon **43**

Popsicle

This popsicle is super cool and the stick adds a nice, realistic touch. You can decorate it however you like—this one is strawberry, orange, and lemon flavored and even has sprinkles! The best part about this project is that it will never melt, and when you squish it, it will bounce right back.

Materials:

Black marker
Sponge
Popsicle stick
Double-sided tape
Puffy paints in pink, yellow, orange, white, and black
Bobby pin
Ball chain (optional)
Label (from page 108)

Tools:

Scissors
Paintbrush

 Draw a rectangle with one curved end onto your sponge.

TIP
You can make your popsicle any shape you like—why not make a bunch of different treats?

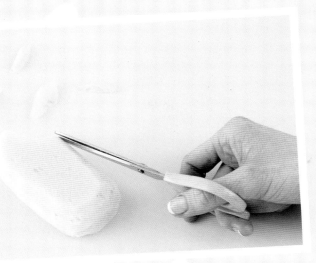

2 Cut it out, then round off the edges to give it a nice smooth finish. Make sure to carve one corner to look like someone took a bite of your treat!

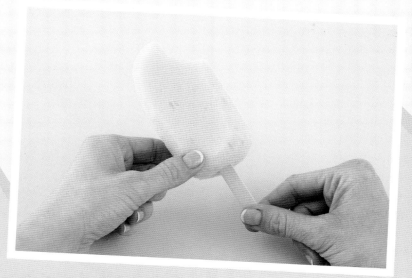

3 Make a slit in the flat bottom of the rectangle, use double-sided tape on your popsicle stick, poke it in, and squeeze to secure.

TURN THE PAGE

4 Use pink, yellow, and orange puffy paint to paint the foam like a layered popsicle. Use white puffy paint to color in the popsicle interior. Once fully dry, add sprinkle details using different puffy paint colors.

5 Next, paint a smiley face on the flat side with black puffy paint. Don't forget to add rosy cheeks!

6 Use tape to attach your label to the ball chain, and then slide the chain into the bobby pin. Push the bobby pin into the sponge to finish.

TIP
For a realistic finish, add drips of puffy paint to make it look like the popsicle's melting.

Grape Ball

The magic of the grape ball is only revealed when squeezed! The mixture in the balloon is pushed through the net to create a bulging bunch of grapes. You can experiment putting different color mixtures in the balloons to make it color changing, or try using a purple balloon for variety.

Materials:

Balloon
1 cup hair conditioner
½ cup baking soda
Fruit net
Cotton thread
Rubber band
Craft foam
Double-sided tape

Tools:

Funnel
Plastic bottle (empty, clean, and dry)
Bowl
Spoon
Scissors

 1 Mix the baking soda and conditioner in the bowl, and use the funnel to pour the ingredients into a bottle. Put the lid on the bottle and shake it up to combine the mixture.

Inflate the balloon slightly and stretch the neck of the balloon over the neck of the bottle. Tip the bottle upside down, and push the paste into the balloon.

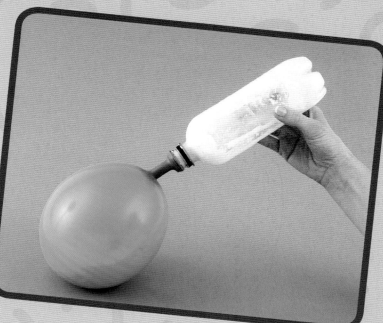

3 Once it is all in, remove the balloon from the bottleneck, release the excess air, and tie a knot at the opening.

TURN THE PAGE

4 Take your piece of net, wrap it around the balloon, and secure it in place using cotton thread and a rubber band. Trim off any excess net.

TIP
Changing the size of the netting will also change the size of the grapes. Try a wider fishing net to make them bigger!

5 Cut the craft foam into a leaf shape and use double-sided tape to attach it to the net. Squeeze to reveal the grapes!

Robot

This project may look hard as metal, but it's actually super soft! They say robots have a great memory; well, this one's made of memory foam. Its slow rise back is especially satisfying. The only technical part is drawing the buttons, but you can get as creative as you like with the details!

Materials:

Black marker
Memory foam
Puffy paints in blue, white, red, yellow, green, and black
Ball chain (optional)
Label (from page 108)
Tape

Tools:

Scissors
Paintbrushes

1

Draw a robot shape onto your memory foam and use the scissors to cut it out, making sure to keep your lines straight.

2

Use blue puffy paint to paint the robot and wait for it to dry.

3 Then, use red puffy paint to color the feet.

4 Use additional paint to add buttons, bolts, and a face.

5 Finally, use tape to attach your label to the ball chain, and then slide the chain into the bobby pin. Push the bobby pin into the memory foam to finish.

SMILEY

Simple yet effective, this iconic yellow smiley is bound to bring a lot of happiness to your day! Satisfyingly smooth, the balloon makes a perfectly round squishy, perfect as the base for a whole collection of emoticons.

Materials:
Yellow balloon
1 cup cornstarch
Black marker

Tools:
Funnel
Plastic bottle (empty, clean, and dry)
Scissors

1

Using the funnel, pour the cornstarch into the bottle.

2

Inflate the balloon slightly and stretch it over the neck of the bottle.

3 Tip the bottle upside down to pour all the cornstarch into the balloon, remove it from the bottle, release the excess air, and tie a knot at the opening.

4

Trim off the balloon excess.

5

Use the black marker to draw eyes and a mouth—use emoticons for inspiration!

TIP!
Why not make a collection of faces with different expressions?

POOP EMOJi

This classic poop is a must-make for any emoji lover; who wouldn't want to squeeze a tiny paper poop?! The basic materials are easy to come by, so there are no excuses not to plop one out. It can make a great key chain or bag accessory, too.

Materials:

White paper
Brown, pink, and black markers or colored pencils
Wide clear tape
Stuffing

Tools:

Scissors

1 Fold your paper in half, draw a poop emoji shape on the folded edge, and color it in.

2 Trace the outline through to the other side of the paper. Color in the back of your design.

3 Unfold your paper, then cover your design in clear tape.

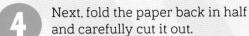

4 Next, fold the paper back in half and carefully cut it out.

5 Tape the edges of the poop emoji together to create a pouch. Leave an opening in the side, so you can stuff it easily.

6 Poke your stuffing into the pouch, and tape up the opening to finish.

Heart

Totally adorable, this heart is the perfect addition to your squishy collection. It's also a great gift for your friends, family, or anyone who makes your heart feel squishy. This one has a blissful smile, but you can get creative with the facial expression you add on. You can make it any size, and the bigger you go, the bigger the squish (just like real life!).

Materials:

Black marker
Memory foam
Puffy paints in pink and black
Bobby pin
Ball chain (optional)
Label (from page 108)
Tape

Tools:

Scissors
Paintbrushes

1 Draw a heart shape onto your memory foam.

2 Cut out the shape and curve the corners, rounding them so they are nice and smooth.

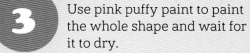

3 Use pink puffy paint to paint the whole shape and wait for it to dry.

4 Use black puffy paint to draw a cute face on it.

5 Once dry, use tape to attach your label to the ball chain, and then slide the chain into the bobby pin. Push the bobby pin into the memory foam to finish.

Brain

The perfect squishy to help you recall memories—as you squeeze you'll be able to think more clearly and de-stress your own brain, too! This memory foam memory brain will be super slow to rise, so you'll be able to see your brain grow back to size after a good squish—so calming!

Materials:

Black marker
Memory foam
Puffy paints in purple and pink
Bobby pin
Ball chain (optional)
Label (from page 109)
Tape

Tools:

Scissors
Paintbrushes

1 Draw a brain shape onto your memory foam.

2 Use the scissors to cut the shape out. Then curve off the corners, and carve the center line to create the two lobes.

3 Use purple puffy paint to cover the whole shape and wait for it to dry.

4 Then, use pink puffy paint to draw wiggles all over to look like brain folds.

To personalize this design, replace the pink wiggles with words and memories that are in your brain instead.

5 Once dry, use tape to attach your label to the ball chain, and then slide the chain into the bobby pin. Push the bobby pin into the memory foam to finish.

CUTE CLOUD

This cute cloud will bring a smile to your day come rain or shine. Using white paper as a base gives it a nice crisp finish, and the simple decoration is easy to draw and alter. You could take it a step further and add multicolored raindrops to the bottom of your cloud.

Materials:

White paper
Black and pink markers or colored pencils
Wide clear tape
Stuffing
Bobby pin
Ball chain (optional)
Label (from page 108)

Tools:

Scissors

1 Fold your paper in half and draw a cloud shape along the fold, adding a cute face in the middle of it—you can get creative and give it cheeks too if you like!

2 Trace the outline through to the back of the paper.

3 Unfold the paper and cover your whole design in clear tape.

4 Fold it back in half and then carefully cut it out.

5 Tape the edges of the cloud together to create a pouch. Leave an opening in the side, so you can stuff it easily.

6 Poke your stuffing into the pouch, and tape up the opening. Leave a small hole for a bobby pin.

7 Use tape to attach your label to the ball chain, then slide the chain into the bobby pin. Poke the pin into the small hole and secure with tape.

RAINBOW

Bringing color to your collection, this squishy little rainbow is a good excuse to use all of your paints at the same time. If you want to take it a step further, you can add glitter to each of the ends for that extra magic touch.

Materials:

Black marker
Memory foam
Puffy paints in red, purple, orange, yellow, green, and blue
Bobby pin
Ball chain (optional)
Label (from page 108)
Tape

Tools:

Scissors
Paintbrushes

1 Draw a rainbow shape onto your memory foam.

2 Cut out the shape, curving off the edges.

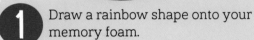

3 Use red puffy paint to paint the top curve, overlapping the edges.

4 Then use purple puffy paint to paint the bottom curve, overlapping the edges.

5 Paint both of the flat sides with curves of orange, yellow, green, and blue puffy paint to complete the rainbow effect.

6 Finally, use tape to attach your label to the ball chain, and then slide the chain into the bobby pin. Push the bobby pin into the memory foam to finish.

CACTUS

It may look spiky, but this cactus is actually super soft and squishy! Its sponge texture gives it a slightly rough finish to look like the skin of the cactus. You can make any shaped cactus you desire—to take it a step further, try adding flowers to the top for an extra cute finish.

Materials:

Black and pink markers
Sponge
Puffy paints in green and yellow
Bobby pin
Ball chain (optional)
Label (from page 108)
Tape

Tools:

Scissors
Paintbrushes

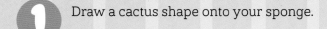

1 Draw a cactus shape onto your sponge.

2 Cut out the shape, then curve off all of the edges to give it a rounded look.

3 Paint the whole shape with green puffy paint. Once fully dry, add dots of yellow puffy paint to look like spikes.

4 Once dry, use a black marker to give it a face, and add cheeks with a pink marker.

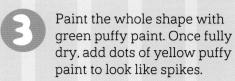

5 Finally, use tape to attach your label to the ball chain, and then slide the chain into the bobby pin. Push the bobby pin into the sponge to finish.

NARWHAL

The unicorn of the ocean, this paper narwhal squishy is fun to make and looks great on a key chain. You can also add all kinds of expressions to it when you color it in. The simple materials mean you can get started right away!

Materials:

White paper
Blue, yellow, pink, and black markers or colored pencils
Wide clear tape
Stuffing
Bobby pin
Ball chain (optional)
Label (from page 108)

Tools:

Scissors

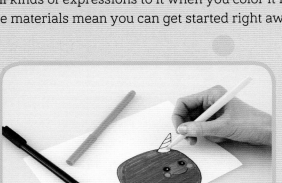

1 Fold your paper in half, draw a cute narwhal shape along the fold line, and then color it in.

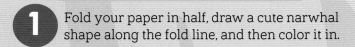

2 Trace the outline through to the other side of the paper. Add details and color to the back of the design.

3 Unfold your paper and cover the design in clear tape.

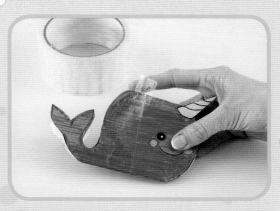

4 Fold it back in half and then carefully cut it out.

5 Tape the edges of the narwhal together to create a pouch. Leave an opening in the side, so you can stuff it easily.

6 Poke your stuffing into the pouch, and tape up the opening. Leave a small hole for a bobby pin.

7 Use tape to attach your label to the ball chain, and then slide the chain into the bobby pin. Poke the bobby pin into the small hole and secure with tape.

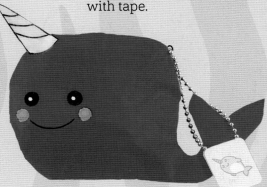

JELLYFiSH

Much more friendly than in real life, this jellyfish is super squishy but without the sting! The main body is a balloon, giving it a perfectly round base and smooth squeeze. You can use any type of plastic bag you like to create the tentacles, although a translucent one gives the most realistic effect.

Materials:

Blue balloon
1 cup cornstarch
Black and pink markers
Clear plastic grocery bag
Rubber band

Tools:

Funnel
Plastic bottle (empty, clean, and dry)
Scissors

1 Using the funnel, pour the cornstarch into the bottle.

2 Inflate the balloon slightly and stretch it over the neck of the bottle.

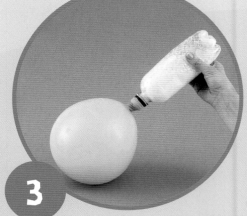

3 Tip the bottle upside down to pour all the cornstarch into the balloon. Remove it from the bottle, release the excess air, and tie a knot at the opening.

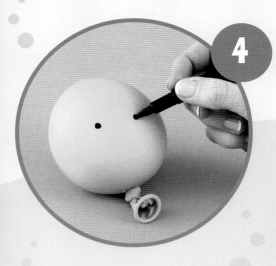

Use the black marker to give it a cute face, and the pink marker to add cheeks.

Cut your grocery bag into a flat piece, and wrap it around the balloon. Secure the bag with a rubber band.

Finally, snip the excess bag into strips to look like tentacles.

Penguin

Everybody loves penguins, especially when they look as cool as this! This one is simple to make; the double balloon covering makes it very durable and satisfying to squish, too. You can give yours any expression—the pink cheeks do make it look extra cute, though.

Materials:
White balloon
Black balloon
1 cup cornstarch
Black, orange, and pink markers

Tools:
Funnel
Plastic bottle (empty, clean, and dry)
Scissors

1 Using the funnel, pour the cornstarch into the bottle.

2 Inflate the white balloon slightly and stretch it over the neck of the bottle.

3 Tip the bottle upside down to pour all of the cornstarch into the balloon. Remove it from the bottle, release the excess air, and tie a knot at the opening.

4 Cut the neck off the black balloon and stretch it over the white balloon.

5 Finally, use the black marker to add a cute face, the orange marker to add a beak and feet, and the pink marker to add cheeks.

Fox

An elegant squishy fox with a curled tail is the perfect addition to your collection. It can be squished and curled to look like a baby cub, and it will grow back to adult size when released. You could take it a step further and make a whole family of them in different poses and sizes, too.

Materials:
Black marker
Memory foam
Puffy paints in orange and white

Tools:
Scissors
Paintbrushes

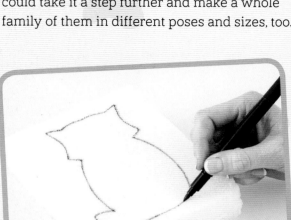

1 Draw the outline shape of a fox onto your memory foam.

2 Use the scissors to carefully cut out the fox shape, and then curve off the edges and smooth them out.

3 Cover the shape with orange puffy paint; leave the face, tummy, and tip of the tail unpainted.

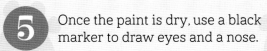

4 Then, use white puffy paint to color the face, the tummy, and the tip of the tail.

5 Once the paint is dry, use a black marker to draw eyes and a nose.

Duck

Based on a classic yellow rubber duck design, this project is simple and quick to make. Using easy-to-find materials, it's perfect for when you need a squishy fast. It looks great on a key chain, and it can be made any size, color, or pattern that you desire!

Materials:

White paper
Yellow, orange, and black markers or colored pencils
Wide clear tape
Stuffing

Tools:

Scissors

1 Fold your paper in half and draw a duck shape along the folded edge, then color it in.

2 Trace the outline through to the other side of the paper, and color in the design.

3 Unfold your paper and cover your design in clear tape.

4 Fold it back in half and then carefully cut it out.

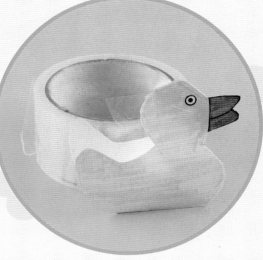

5 Tape the edges of the duck together to create a pouch. Leave an opening in one of the sides so you can stuff it easily.

6 Now it's time to stuff your squishy! Poke your stuffing into the pouch, and tape up the opening to finish.

Tortoise

This super sweet little tortoise is made from sponge, giving its shell a realistic finish. You can decorate the shell however you like. This one has hexagonal patterns with dots, but there is nothing stopping you from giving it your own spin. You can have fun squishing his body and watching his head pop out of the shell!

Materials:

Black marker
Sponge
Puffy paints in green, red, pink, and black
Bobby pin
Ball chain (optional)
Label (from page 109)
Tape

Tools:

Scissors
Paintbrushes

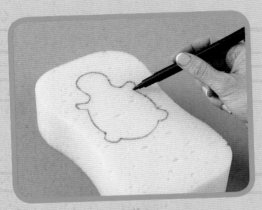

1 Draw the outline shape of a tortoise onto your sponge.

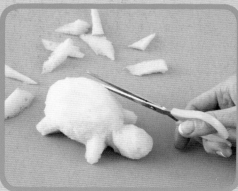

2 Carefully cut it out, curve off the edges, and shape them with the scissors.

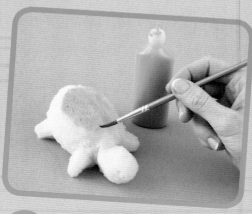

3 Use green puffy paint to paint the shell.

4 Then, mix green and red puffy paint to make a brown color; use this to cover the head and limbs, and leave to dry.

5 Once dry, use black puffy paint to give the tortoise a smiley face and the pink puffy paint to give him cheeks. Then, decorate his shell with additional puffy paint.

6 Finally, use tape to attach your label to the ball chain, and then slide the chain into the bobby pin. Push the bobby pin into the sponge.

BEAR

This smooth squishy has a satisfying squish and is totally adorable. You may be able to find a balloon that is already bear shaped, and you can decorate it however you like. Why not make a whole family of of squishy bears?

Materials:
Gold balloon
1 cup cornstarch
Black and pink markers

Tools:
Funnel
Plastic bottle (empty, clean, and dry)
Scissors

1 Using the funnel, pour the cornstarch into the bottle.

2 Inflate the balloon slightly and stretch it over the neck of the bottle.

Use any colored balloon you like—your bear doesn't have to be realistic!

3 Tip the bottle upside down to pour all of the cornstarch into the balloon. Remove it from the bottle, release the excess air, and tie a knot at the opening.

4 Trim off the balloon excess.

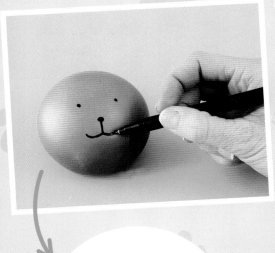

5 Use the black marker to draw the eyes, nose, mouth, and ears, and the pink marker for additional details.

How to Make Slime

Fluffy Unicorn "Milkshake"

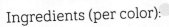

This ultimate, colorful slime "shake" is a sure way to impress your friends. As you play with it the colors will merge, creating a wonderful swirly pattern, just like unicorn magic! You can also add glitter to give it an extra sparkle, and store it in a plastic cup to complete the look.

Ingredients (per color):

⅔ cup white glue
2 tbsp shaving cream
4 drops food coloring
1 tsp baking soda
2 tsp contact lens solution
Glitter
Plastic cup

Tools:

Bowl
Spoon

1 Pour the glue into the bowl, squirt in the shaving cream followed by the food dye, and mix well.

2 Add the baking soda and stir the ingredients.

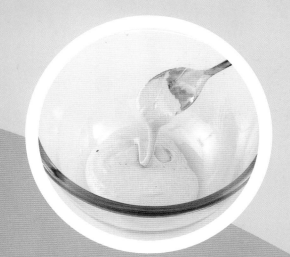

The colors will combine, so make sure you use ones that will blend well.

3 Then, slowly mix in the contact lens solution. Once it starts to come away from the sides of the bowl, knead the slime into a smooth ball. If your mixture is too sticky, just add more contact lens solution. Put it to the side.

4 Repeat the process so you have two or three more colors; you can leave one white for the creamy milkshake topping.

5 Stretch the colors out and mix them to create a magical unicorn fluffy slime. Put it into your cup. Add the white slime on top, and sprinkle on the glitter.

Fluffy Unicorn "Milkshake"   **85**

FRIED EGG SLIME

A fun favorite, this satisfying slime looks just like the real thing! As you play with it, the colors will scramble, to look like an equally appealing egg dish. Why not make a "toast" squishy, too, using a sponge and puffy paint? That'll really complete your breakfast!

Materials (per color):
⅔ cup white glue
1 tbsp shaving cream
4 drops yellow food coloring
1 tsp baking soda
1 tsp contact lens solution

Tools:
Bowl
Spoon

1 Pour the glue into the bowl and squirt in the shaving cream. Add the baking soda and stir everything together.

2 Slowly mix in the contact lens solution. Once it starts to come away from the sides of the bowl, knead the slime into a smooth ball. If your mixture is too sticky, just add more contact lens solution. This will be your egg white. Put it to the side.

3 Repeat the process, and add yellow food coloring into the glue. This will be the egg yolk.

4 Take a blob of your yellow slime and place it on your white slime to create your fried egg.

Try your egg scrambled!

Metallic Slime

Mesmerizing and magical, this metallic slime looks almost like molten metal—except this is totally safe to play with! The glitter gives it an extra sparkle—you can use as much or as little as you like. You can experiment with different paints to make a range of different metals, such as silver or rose gold.

Materials:
⅔ cup clear glue
Gold paint
Fine gold glitter
1 tsp baking soda
1 tsp contact lens solution

Tools:
Bowl

1 Pour the glue into the bowl, then add the gold paint and glitter.

2 Add the baking soda and stir the ingredients together.

3

Slowly mix in the contact lens solution. Once it starts to come away from the sides of the bowl, knead the slime into a smooth ball. If your mixture is too sticky, just add more contact lens solution.

4

Roll in more glitter to intensify the shine.

MAGNETIC SLIME

ZAP!

Science at its finest—this slime is totally unreal! The iron oxide in it is what makes it magnetic and gives it its intense color. You can have lots of fun seeing quite how far you can get yours to stretch just with the power of a magnet.

Ingredients:

⅔ cup white glue
4 tbsp iron oxide powder
Fine white glitter
1 tsp baking soda
1 tsp contact lens solution
Googly eyes (optional)

Tools:

Spoon
Bowl
Magnet
Gloves

1 Pour the glue into the bowl. Stir in the iron oxide powder, 1 tbsp of fine glitter, and the baking soda.

2 Slowly stir in the contact lens solution using a spoon. If the mixture is too sticky, add more contact lens solution.

3 Roll in more glitter and use your magnet to manipulate the slime and pull it into different shapes.

TIP!

Turn your slime into a monster by adding googly eyes—then watch it consume the magnet!

SAFETY!

Use iron oxide powder with caution. It can cause coughing and respiratory problems. Replace it with iron filings if you are concerned. Wear a mask and wash your hands thoroughly after mixing the slime.

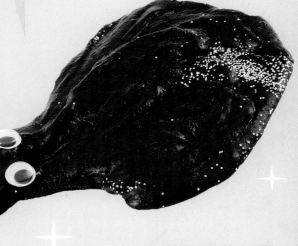

Magnetic Slime

Jello Slime

Realistic, wobbly, and super slimy, this incredible jello slime is translucent just like the real thing. You can adapt it by changing the color or adding pom-poms into the mix. To take it an extra step further, why not add a couple of drops of fragrance to make it scented?

Materials:

1¼ cups clear glue
4 drops food coloring
1 tbsp baking soda
1 tbsp contact lens solution
Oil, for lining the jello mold

Tools:

Spoon
Bowl
Jello mold

1 Pour the glue into the bowl. Stir in the food coloring and baking soda.

2 Slowly stir in the contact lens solution. Mix the slime with your hands. If the mixture is too sticky, add more contact lens solution.

3 Rub a small amount of oil around the jello mold, then place the slime inside, and flip the mold upside down. Lift it off the slime and watch as the slime melts!

TOP TIP!

Repeat the process with different colors to make a layered jello.

How to Make Putty

FARTING PUTTY

A comedy classic, this silly putty will have you and your friends in giggles for hours with the rude noises it can produce. The key here is to find the perfect pot to squish it in; this also means you can keep it with you on the go, leading to hilarious situations!

Materials:
⅔ cup white glue
4 drops food coloring
1 tbsp baking soda
2 tbsp cornstarch
1 tbsp contact lens solution

Tools:
Spoon
Bowl
Plastic pot

1 Pour the glue into the bowl. Stir in the food coloring, baking soda, and cornstarch.

2 Slowly stir in the contact lens solution. Mix the putty with your hands. If the mixture is too sticky, add more contact lens solution.

3 Put the putty into the pot, making sure air is trapped underneath. Push the putty down with your fingers to make hilarious noises that will never grow old!

Playdough Putty

An absolute classic, this is a great recipe for making a standard playdough. Easy to make, you'll be able to sculpt for hours with this putty, especially if you repeat the process to create it in many colors. There really will be no limit to what you can make!

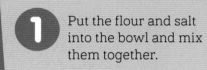

Materials:

1 cup flour
½ cup salt
1 tbsp oil
4 drops food coloring
½ cup water

Tools:

Spoon
Bowl

1 Put the flour and salt into the bowl and mix them together.

2 Add the oil, water, and food coloring, and stir really well! If it's too sticky, add more flour; if it's too dry, add more water.

3 Knead the dough into a smooth ball and you're ready to play!

Bath-Time Putty

Good clean fun! This putty is great for playing with in the bathtub and for keeping you sparkly clean. You can use any type of shower gel or body wash, and add anything from glitter to fragrances to really make it your own. This makes a great gift for friends and family.

Materials:

1 cup cornstarch
1 cup shower gel or body wash
4 drops food coloring
1 tbsp oil
Glitter

Tools:

Spoon
Bowl

 1 Put the cornstarch in the bowl, followed by the shower gel, food coloring, glitter, and oil.

2 Stir all of the ingredients together.

3 Then, knead the putty into a ball. If it's too dry, add more shower gel; if it's too wet, add more cornstarch. Break off a small amount to play with in the bathtub!

Anti-Stress Putty

The perfect way to unwind is with this calming anti-stress putty—fun to squeeze, pull, and poke, it is easy to make, will keep you occupied for hours, and will take your mind off of your worries. You can make it any color you like, and add calming fragrances to totally chill you out.

Materials:

1 cup flour
½ cup salt
3 tbsp cream of tartar
1 tbsp oil
½ cup warm water
4 drops food coloring
Glitter (optional)
Lavender oil (optional)

Tools:

Spoon
Bowl

1 Put the flour, salt, and cream of tartar into the bowl.

2

Mix in the oil, warm water, and food coloring.

3

Then, knead the putty into a ball. If it's too sticky, add more flour; if it's too dry, add more water Add the glitter and lavender oil if you like, and to knead to combine.

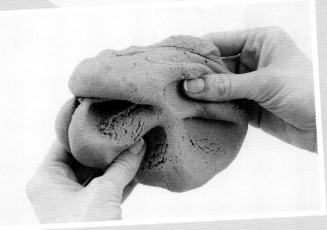

Snowman Putty

Materials:

1 cup white glue
½ cup shaving cream
2 tbsp baking soda
2 tbsp baby oil
4 tbsp cornstarch
2 tsp contact lens solution
2 small twigs
2 googly eyes
1 small orange craft foam triangle

Tools:

Spoon
Bowl

The magic of this putty is in the melt. Once you've made your putty, sculpt it into a snowman shape and then watch in awe as it melts into a puddle. The best part is that you can repeat the process again and again with the same putty—without any mess!

1 Put the glue, shaving cream, and baking soda into the bowl, and then stir the ingredients together.

2 Mix in the baby oil, then the cornstarch.

3

Slowly stir in the contact lens solution. Then, mix the putty with your hands; if the mixture is too sticky, add more contact lens solution.

TURN THE PAGE

4 It's time to build your snowman! Split your putty to make one big ball for the body and one smaller ball for the head.

5 Place the smaller ball on top of the bigger ball, and then decorate your snowman with twigs, eyes, and a craft foam nose.

Watch him melt!

Labels and Packaging

Give your squishies a professional touch with labels and packaging. Cut out the labels from the book or trace over them to design your own! See page 14 for instructions on how to attach labels to your squishies.

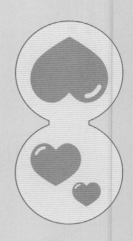

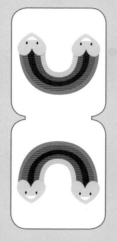

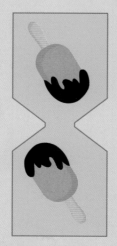

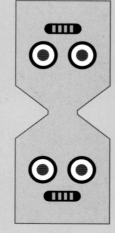

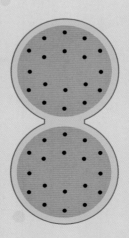

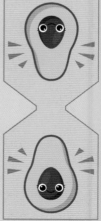

Boxes

Use the template below to make boxes for your squishies. Simply adjust the size to fit your squishy. Cut out the square, draw a smaller square inside it, and score the lines of it using a closed pair of scissors. Cut from the outer edge to each corner of the inner square and fold up the sides. Secure using double-sided tape or a glue stick.

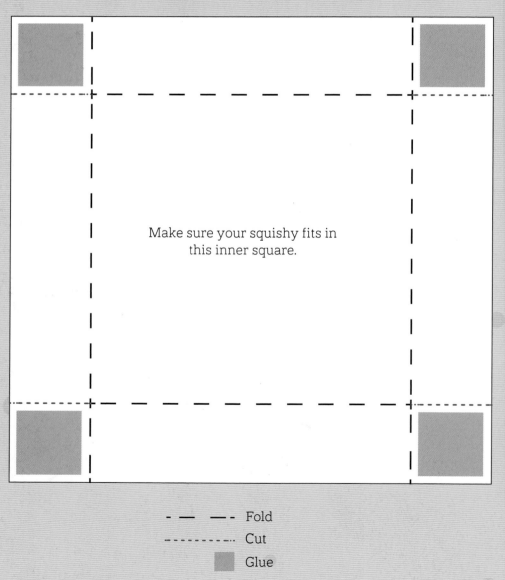

Make sure your squishy fits in this inner square.

- — —- Fold

--------- Cut

Glue

Why not try using colorful or patterned card paper to make your box look even more professional?

Happy Squishing!

About the Author

Tessa Sillars-Powell is a professional crafter who works in television and publishing, teaching the world how to make wondrous things.

She believes there is nothing more satisfying than inspiring creativity and giving people the confidence to get messy. Always looking out for the latest craft crazes, Tessa has a passion for experimenting, trying new materials and methods, and making projects that everyone can understand and get involved with—whatever their skill level.

With a plan always in mind and her craft cupboard constantly bursting, Tessa has always liked making things for her friends and family and is over the moon to be able to share these ideas with you.

Tessa lives in London in a higgledy-piggledy house with a cat named Rio.